GLIMPSES

Sarah Drury

Sarah Drury

Drury, Sarah
1st edition
ISBN: 9798470690418

"Some beautiful paths can't be discovered without getting lost."

~ Erol Ozan

Sarah Drury

A HUNDRED AND FIFTY METRES

Must've been a year,
Or more,
Since the stench of Chlorine
Kissed our noses like
A bleach infused slap
From a scrubber's palm.

Think my cossie was having
A laugh.
Lumps where there shouldn't
Be bumps and
I only eat cake if there's
A 'y' in the day of the week.

Welcomed by the water
As its own.
This leisure dome,
Pleasure dome.
Two parts hydrogen,
One part oxygen.
And you had not forgotten.
And you had not slipped
Its memory either.

There could have been a hundred
Bodies in that pool,
Choking in huddles,
Like pilchards in a tin.
You cut through them all,
With your sleek, slim grace,
And your immaculate front crawl.

Deep ends worry me,
Because in my memory
You are five and
I'm fearful of how you'd survive.
But you're thirteen.

But you glide and
You glide and
You glide.
And a hundred and fifty metres
was not a distance.

It was a knighthood.

ABSTRACT DAD

It's a long time,
Fifty-one years minus 7,
For 'dad' to be
An abstract concept.
The one photo
Pretends, from a frame,
That we remember each other,
And it feels unnerving,
Gazes meeting in
Cognition of
Memories never
Made.

I have modelled
My own men.
Collaged works
Of art from
Movies and books,
Myths and magic.
Perfect.
And each one bears
A heart shaped
Like you,
Dad.

BACH

I try to describe how it feels.
Bach.
As the beauty flows through me,
Like a gentle orgasm,
But ghost fingered
And subtle.
Take me to heaven,
Caressed by quavers
And smooth legatos.
Play fiddles on
My vulnerability.
So reliable, so predictable.
I waltz in threes with
The metronome,
Dictating the pulse
Of the annuls of time.
The comfort holds me
Like the arms of
A beloved soulmate,
As rapture possesses
My hungry soul.
I die again.
Then gasp in breaths
Of ebb and flow,
As I lose my senses.
Yet I find myself
In Utopia.
Once more.

B

It would be too easy
To shuffle past.
Head down,
Lips glued fast,
Or to judge.

But…
You'd borrowed
The eyes of an angel,
Peering out from
A voile of dirt
And disarray.
A drug fuelled haze
Dissolved the intimacy
Away.

"I am human,
I deserve to be loved",
In childish font on a
Torn-box manuscript.
And my eyes
Betray my heart.
You blame yourself
On yourself,
And I stand here
Frozen lipped.

Like an apology,
You tell tales
Of sleeping in a bin,
Every night,
And I can't put this right.

And I can't
Put hope in your heart.
Because I don't lie.
And my words are
Empty promises.

I dissolve into
The nonchalant crowds,
And I cry.

BIG WORDS

You tripped over your tongue today.
Big words falling from youthful lips.
Too big for you, boy.
It's the teenage hormones,
They tell me.
I say you're just
Being a little shit.
But people in glass houses
Shouldn't throw stones.

Sarah Drury

CACOPHONY IN CLEETHORPES

We move like filleted haddock.
White, pasty, hasty,
Jostling into tumble, bumble, stumbles,
Boneless beneath this sea of skeletons.

It is a busy busyness,
As the Summer sighs its
Last shimmers of a warm lung languish.
Soon, Winter will drift down upon the
Neon-light sands,
Pilfering the bustling flow
Of carefree humanity.

But now we play,
In swathes of glowing, heat-tinged day,
Children with their sticky teeth, smiling
Through candyfloss halos,
Dentists wringing hands
And counting crumbling cavities.

And the whole world feasting
On haddock and chips,
Snapping gnasher jaws
And slippery chip-fat fingertips.

Clutching well-worn tuppenny pieces,
Faces lit like sparkler moonbeams,
Ears buzzing with cacophony,
The seek-a-high kids cavort with the thrill
Of the addict gamble,
As they listen for the cascading tumble
Of their millionaire win,

And shrieks slice through
The forced grown-up grimaces
Of too-long days out.

Tired children slumber,
Weary bones dragged over
Homebound wheels,
And into sugar dreams,
And happy ever afters.

DAYS

Days like these.
When I am alone.
When the sky feels defeated
By monochromatic dissonance,
Yet I see beyond,
To its splendid azure hesitance.

Messiah flowing through
Peace time ethers.
And I don't know these strangers,
But they know my soul.
And I feel I could
Be uplifted no more.
That I am chewing
Morsels of heaven.
Dainty tastes of
Eloquence.
Largo. Andante. Moderato,
And the music
Settles on my
Comforted soul,
In the manner
That untainted snow paints
Ivory blanket amnesty
Over the spilled bloods
Of troubled soils.

When friends are
Just there.
Linking lives and
Spending words
Like a care culture currency.

When I wear my birth rite face,
Without a self-conscious care.
When I don't care that
Negligence is nesting in my hair.
I feel free.
And I am me,
For now.

MISSING YOU

As the warm,
Comforting glow of
Yuletide shenanigans,
Wraps itself around
My melted heart.
As the last candle on
The mantel,
Sings a soliloquy and
Melts into new
Incarnations of its waxy self,
And the ten years since you
Rendezvoused with
The light side,
I see your chair,
All empty there.
Missing you.

That last Christmas,
Heaven knew
That the angel of time
Was pausing
Her inhibiting breath,
Whilst you cherished your last.
We gasped those last months
In expanses of
winterscape lungs,
And I don't know
But I'm sure the universe
Painted our visions
Titanium white,
What with the snow and
Cerulean, stark winter sun skies.

I see the space in our bed,
The place where, once,
You were mortal,
All empty there.
Missing you.

I knew you'd be here,
And you were,
Amidst the shreds of gaudy
And rips of tearing carnage.
Presents from a widow's
Best efforts.
Brave smiles, well-rehearsed.
After ten years of
Xmas dinners for two,
And only one grown-up
At the table.
Playing secret Santa
And making all the
Responsibilities
Look easy.
There should've been
Frolicking with crackers,
And snapping away
Our feigned hilarity,
As we tossed lame jokes
Into joyous memories.
But turkey is for two
Now.
Your plate all empty there.
Missing you.

Sarah Drury

FABERGE

Don't know
How I feel today,
Really.
Like a Faberge egg,
Without
Its decadence.
A single, precarious
Tongue could
Crush my shell,
Though I am held
In esteem
By quicksilver
Minds and
Moods.
Permanence and
Providence
Taunt me
With their
Translucency,
But,
My skin is thin
And let's all the
Nonsense in,
When there
Is little room
For inadequacy.

FLAT

Feel a little flat today,
But hoisting up
My big girl pants.
Flat seems smooth,
And smooth seems better
Than jagged edges.
I don't want to
Cut myself on tears
Today.

I paint poppies,
They spit at me.
All vehemence
And blood red petals.
Earthy stems.
I envy their connection
To the Earth,
And write eulogies
For my disconnection.

Thank god
Music
Is like a loving mother
Who sings to me.
Paints my platitude.
All those notes,
squeezed into colours,
And carefully
Conforming.
Want today to be a rainbow.
Want to gaze
Through kaleidoscopes.

Not nonchalant eyes.

FOR CHRISTMAS

I know what you want
For Christmas, son.
Your dad.
But death's not easy like that,
Heaven has no returns policy,
And I hate
That life has made you so sad.
If I could bring back
Daddy I would be glad,
Gladder,
Gladdest.
Don't you think
It rips my heart out,
To see my son the saddest,
When the sun rises
On Christmas morning
To the chime of
Yuletide bells,
And it's another one
Of those
'missing you like hell'
Times.
There's nothing in
My heart that can
Conjure up rhymes
For the pain you feel.
You don't like my poems,
Anyhow,
You've heard all my speil.
You'll have to
Make do with me, Kiddo.
I can't tell you

What testosterone feels like,
But I can whisper
In eulogies of
I love you.

GHOST OF A FEATHER

Here I am.
Fifty-one years old.
Juggling with a thousand
Iron-plumed swallows,
Whilst struggling to lift up
The ghost of a feather.

My tears.
Drops of saline fears.
Diamonds drowning shadows
Of harrowing spectres of
Lion-hearted years.
My mind gifts itself to the
Lunacy of the moon,
And the sun sets on my sanity.

I am all sincere smiles,
Painted over
Old, cracked plaster.
Gaudy reds flake off chalky lips.
Words, exhausted with the
Work of holding up hearts.
Do my eyes speak?
Or do they whisper?
All apologies and tangled lashes?

Here I am,
juggling nerves of steel
With prescriptions for Valium.
Whilst struggling to lift up
The weight of a dying breath.

GHOST

Did you ever notice
My come-to-me eyes?
All weeping willows
And rainy Sundays.
Heavy with the hoodwinked vision
Of premonition and
Cupid's mindless wisdom.
Aiming arrows at anarchy.
Making myths of
Mothers and martyrs.

I sang to you
In lipless psalms.
My serenades birthed nightingales
From the womb of nightmares.
Sonnets equate summertime storms
In silence
When they echo
Off ricochet hearts.
You sounded so holy,
Children cascading from your
Teacher's tongue.
You'd toss a sunrise smile,
As the suicide sun set in sinful sighs,
And I knew I
Could never be the one.

Kisses die when they
Melt onto phantom lips.
I choked on my counterfeit lungs
And gouged myself on feasts
Of avocado and asphyxiation.

All mournful cries and
Generic white sheets.
I was a ghost
In your disbelief.
My heart,
A spectre.

GLASS JAR

Sometimes I wish that
Hearts were like spiders,
And I could trap yours
In a pretty glass jar.
I would gaze all day,
Contemplating reasons you should stay,
And we would sleep silently together,
Under a duvet of opalescent stars.

Arachnids move so fast,
And I don't want you to
Move at all.
I am so tired of loving from a distance.
You are oblivious to the longing
In the rise and fall
Of my half heart hope.
I want to gaze in awe.
As you weave your spun silk webs,
To grace the gardens of my metaphor.
Mine only.

I would covet your little glass house,
Cup my loving hands around the
Fragile glass.
Sense the lukewarm flesh and bones
Of my unrequited, taboo lass.
No escaping my love,
In your little, crystal prison.
The fireflies would cry by the dark
Of the night,
And the moon would whisper secrets,
When the trusting sun had risen,

And no-one would hear,
But the universe would listen.
And our hearts.

GORECKI

I put Gorecki on
The CD player today.
Wanted to reward myself
After the mundane drudgery.
House sparkling clean,
I felt like a queen,
Where the servants have
Embraced anarchy, and
Severed their chains
of subordinance.

Gorecki,
Smooth and deep,
Going nowhere and maybe that's why
I love it.
The music floats, ethereal,
Like dandelions, lost
On a soft spring breeze.
I don't even know what the
Singer is singing,
But the notes whisper glimpses
Of seduction,
Into my ears.
This faceless lady
Who seems to reach
Into the complexities
Of my soul.

And all the sadness
Seeps into oblivion,
Painting soliloquies
In brilliant, sunshine days.

But the joy,
Oh, the joy.
I can't describe how
Magnanimous the
Splendour.
I Live there, a moment,
Cocooned by
The gossamer, feather like
Caresses of angels,
As my soul
Basks in the realms
Of the heaven they call
Euphoria, escape, and freedom.

HOME ED

I was a seventies kid.
It wasn't like this.
Boring books and chalky blackboards,
Glazing analogue eyes, inducing
Spank-your-ass compliance.
Our world didn't perpetually spin
On the axis of a silicon chip.

You are twenty-four hour triggered.
Incessantly wired to some sort
Of teen tech grid.
Living the blue screen dream,
Keep the downloads clean.
Social media,
Fake friends.
People are not always who they seem,
You know.
And you don't.

And it's really hard.
For I'm trying to connect and
Your emotional WiFi denies.
I see the disconnection in your eyes.
I desperately analyse
Where the on switch is.

You say you hate school.
And here we are.
Home ed in Syria.
At war.
Or maybe I'm holding
The wrong weapons.

Autism shouldn't be
Like this.
Bombs tear strips from amnesty tongues,
And all strangers see,
Is child prodigy.
And Rainman.

INDIGO

Indigo blue,
Inky canvas.
Watercolour to my soul of hues.
My slumber-time psyche,
Dormant for hours,
Opens one somnolent eye,
And reticently closes the other.
Melancholy, perchance,
Today will colour the ether black.
Hades snapping at my heels,
Reeking of the stench of apathy.
Foxtrot with feet in asphalt,
Silent, becalmed.
Take my heart, transmute my tears,
Reverie cascading in miniature shards.
Empty aspirations take me beneath
sorrowful, sanguine waters.
A thousand pure white lilies
Falling at my feet,
As I mourn the elegy
Of a smile.

LETTUCE

There's a lettuce
In my fridge.
Lodging two weeks since.
Crispy vigour gone,
Now aged, browning leaves
Are limp-limbed faux apologies.

I look at it every day,
But oh, the apathy.
To nurture it in my
Gluttonous hand
Would kill me.
My lips have cast aversions
On the fresh
And green nutrition,
Lest it smite my greedy penchant
For the sugar high delicious.

My aspirations are genuine.
But perhaps I'm out
To impress the
Delivery man.
With my tomato taunts,
My cucumber come-to-me's
And my lettuce lies.
LIES!

Good intentions,
Bought no biscuits.
Now this broken promise
Mocks me from
Its polar haven.

Into the bin it goes.
It'll never reach its full potential.
Underachiever.
Loser.
It was born to die.

LITTLE BIRD

Little bird,
Is it ok for me to fly now?
I see you there,
All freedom wings and liberty feathers.
I press my face toward the frost-nose window,
And envy that the sky celebrates your name,
That the earth rejoices in your anonymity.
The stigma of my lithium blood,
Clings to me,
Whilst the trauma of my Valium veins,
Purges me.
I am graced with words, they say,
And I feel humbled and blessed,
But if I could write myself into
A new story,
Where my mind basked in dreams
Of peaceful sanctity,
And my chains were shattered
With emancipated ferocity...

My tale will
Never be a New York Times best seller,
And that's ok.
For autographs would be wearisome,
And book launches
Are best left to divas.

And little birds
Who fly.

LITTLE SWITZ

It was a wonderful sort of day.
So cold, the air was misting
Smoke plumes of its
Own breath.
So cold,
The cadavers needed
No mortuaries
For their sordid death.
The sky had been on
The Sertraline again.
Pharmaceutical watercolours
Making pretty pictures
Of the pain.
The ground had set
Like broken bones,
Glinting accusingly
At the sun,
And we were rushing
Into the bright light,
With the stereo blasting,
No sunglasses on.

My breath felt like stalactites,
Stinging fissures in crystalline lungs.
We held hands,
Breaking into
Something someone, somewhere,
Had optimistically sung.
I could've sung you a song,
But I didn't know the ending yet.
I've sung the usuals,
Sad ones, love ones,

But now you were ill
And my tongue was
All goodbye pain and forlorn regret.

Ten years have gone.
My arms are empty and
I've been flying solo.
You've been gone a while,
And the world punches me
Like Mohammed Ali,
But my reactions are too slow.
I'm not the heir to the throne.
But I get up again.
Like the slaughter
To the lamb.
And dust off my crown,
Like the queen
You always said
That I am.

Sarah Drury

LOCKDOWN BIRTHDAY

There's a teenager in the house,
Now.
Feels like thirteen years
Since Covid breathed
In murders of masks and
Hand sanitiser.
Lockdown birthday.
Country cossetted
In an incompetent blanket
Of Westminster restrictions.

Traded an apple for the teacher
For a fortnight in isolation.
I did my best, son.
Pretty pile of presents
Jousting with the garish paper.
You were polite.
All toothpaste smiles and Hollywood thank you's.
That PlayStation slipped your grasp.
Disappointment tarted up with
Gracious teeth and temperate zones.

No fancy parties.
Nowhere open and
We're only allowed to breathe
In sterile bubbles.
The saddest three I've counted
On amputated no-hands.
Papa John's pizza,
Pepsi Max.
Tummies full of Italy,
And the sweet red tang of

The Mediterranean.

We did the cake,
Candles outshined austerity
In this dim-souled era.
Your face shimmered.
Golden when we're in the times of nickel.
I was warm with the glow of it all.
And you, you shone.

LUNAR

Only the moon knows my name,
As she whispers in glitter-lung silver
To the somnolent stars.
I don't want the sun to hear,
With his loose, burnt ember tongue,
And desert lips.
I fear for my anonymity.

Only the moon knows my name.
The waltzes and tangoes of lunacy
Dance upon my lithium feet.
The moon wears my insanity
Like a sinless confession.
I fall to my knees
And confess.
My prayers
Glisten in whispers
Of indanthrene blue.

Only the moon knows my name,
As the tides toy with the moonlit sea.
She wants to promise my name to the ocean,
But I know it will drown.
I dance with shipwrecks
And skeletal sailors,
As I gaze in reflections
At my own mortality,
And the water laughs.

Only the moon knows my name.
And she cherishes her silvery secret,
Nestled between the firefly stars,

And I trust.

Sarah Drury

MARY

You stand there,
All Faberge.
Peace bleeding out of
The corners of your
Speak no evil mouth.
Aura promising a tsunami
Of miracles
As I feel you.
I feel you.

I don't want to adult
Anymore.
I want to be the child
That drowns in merciful swathes
Of your loving compassion.
Swallowed by seas
Of blue silk and chiffon,
As you stroke my rosy cheek
With dove-kiss fingers.

I want to pray,
To resonate the room
With Hail Mary's.
And pass it on,
My pain.
Pass it on to this
Crumbling plaster effigy
With the disintegrating crown
Of decaying gold.
False. Cheap. Lifeless.

I don't know where

42

To put the greatness of my pain.
I've knelt in
Tombstone churches,
Beat my heart with
Crucifixes.
I've paced the streets
With 'sorry son' psalms,
And doors closing
In irritating faces.
But empty is my cup.

You may gaze upon
My pleading, bleeding face,
With your empty eyes
And vacuous ears.
But I know you're there,
Mary.
I feel you.
I feel you.

MERMAID

I never dreamt for I
To fall into the perilous sea,
Of your luminous, ocean eyes.
Beguiled by the ebb and flow of the
Opulent, moonshine, lunar tide.
Maritime mistress,
With your sanguine songs of the sea.
I, a celestial being,
Mesmerised by the lilt and tilt of
Your mermaid tongue,
In tones of cerulean blue,
And longing,
Clothed in depths of aquamarine.

You wanted to toss your iridescent tail
Into heady, celestial spheres.
And here I was, an angel,
Swallowing briny lungfuls
Of sinking ships and sailors.
We made our ascent,
Two mavericks meandering
Through the sunset sky,
Wings flailing in barnacles and flotsam,
Your mythical tail,
Reflecting the perilous waves,
Waxing and waning with the
Moon's magnetic tide.

We were an incongruent pair.
You with your ocean heart,
And I with my Seraphim wings.
You gave Heaven the gift of the oceans,

I gave the gift of the sky, and the earth,
To the sea.

MIDNIGHT

All the mice and men are sleeping.
All breathy, rising chests which fall
Like Autumn ghosts,
And you, for once,
Are peaceful.
Your head, kissing your pillow
With peace talks and
Amnesty.
I need it.

Heaven holds me in its grace,
When the light is low
And the moon is high,
And I am partial to lunacy.
Mother is closed now, for the day,
I love you, baby boy,
And we cry rainbow kaleidoscopes into the sky,
Together.
But
Sometimes I need a break.
I am exhausted,
And my lungs are weary
With the deafening sound of my own silence,
But to breathe is to think
And
I need to create.

I am always last in the race.
But in these twilight hours,
When the sun reveres
The silver tang of a moonlit world,
It really doesn't matter

If I lose.

Sarah Drury

HEARTS

Ten years
Has my heart been
Slumbering in beds of
Somnolent roses.
All pink and dewy and tender,
And half asleep.
I didn't intend to nap
For so long,
But the peace was
Heaven, and
Why wake when
Dreams paint such
Sweet, pastel visuals
On my iniquity?

If I see through my heart,
Then there are
No shadows.
Only the softest
Of glimmers
From a moonlit
Sea of
Ethereal emotions.
And if I hear?
Then dissonance
Has no hope amidst the
Resounding clamour
Of clandestine whispers.

And if I feel?
Then I reign with Neptune
In the realm

Of the ocean,
And my senses are
My promise and
My passions are
A premise

And
My heart
Is a gift.

OLD LADY

You were 83,
And immediately I
Asked you about the war,
As if you were
An historical relic.
And I had visions of
Women painting
Stocking seams on legs,
And cans of Spam,
And dating an
American man.
But you were only
A kid.

You said you were lonely,
And you only
Came out to be
Amongst people,
And I realised
You were a church
Without a steeple,
As you pray
For souls,
For your empty days
To be made whole,
By the passers-by,
And bus stop dwellers,
And anyone who
Has a pulse.

To be thanked for
Loosening my tongue,

And sitting a while
In a dual of 'am'
And 'was' and 'maybe one day',
Sort of makes you
Feel bad.
This old lady, sad,
And happy,
Ricocheting fragments
Of a lonely life
Onto a mirror of
Empathy.
Beaming for the camera
That captures
Brave smiles,
And then putting away
Her lips,
As she doesn't need them
When she gets home
To herself.

ORIGAMI

It is not easy
Being so sentient
In an anaesthetised world.
I try and fold my feelings
Into little origami ships,
Hope they will sail
Nonchalantly into
A world where
Life doesn't sting,
Anymore.

I can pretend it
Doesn't hurt,
Pretend I have a
Heart of polished granite.
I can pretend that feelings
Must only feel like
Fireworks in the
New year's sky,
That to feel is
To loiter somewhere
On a permanent,
Spiritual high.

But I know
To be real
I need to feel
The stain
Of salt kissed tears,
To sing the pain
As it washes through.
It never stays.

And I know I am there,
Sometimes.
Origami ships are fragile,
And my skin is like
Tissue paper,
And I absorb
The world at times,
And it can be too much.
Sometimes.

But,
It never stays.

POPPIES

Our two hands, entwined.
You don't often grace me with your silence.
But today, ten million poppies bleed.
As they died,
these heroes of men.
In fields of fortitude and flowers.
With wives and mothers.
Sisters and brothers.
Children.
Lovers.

Today,
Scarlet paints a promise
On our hearts.
You stand there,
In the image of your soldier father.
All gallantry and valiance.
And my heart defies my eyes.

I never asked you to stand beside me.
'Respect the dead', you said.
And you did.
And I wept.

Our two hands, entwined.
You don't often grace me with your silence.
But today, ten million poppies bleed.

PUZZLED

Do you ever wake up
And feel you're scattered
Over a vast expanse?
Like an old, discarded, wooden jigsaw.
Glass shard feelings,
Smeared like butter,
On the mouldered bread of
A no man's land.

And all the pieces are anomalies,
Too bold,
Too cold,
Too grandiose,
You can't make them fit,
You can't force them,
Like a square peg
In the round hole that
You are.

You have all
The pieces you need,
But you cannot
Fashion them into
Coherent pictures,
And the images play
In sequences that
Have no order,
Have no meaning.
Like a seedy, arthouse movie,
Or a pretentious piece
Of conceptual art.

Maybe life is
Just like that.
Incoherent.
Just is.

RAIN

And so, the rain
Falls again today.
Feel like I'm living beneath
A colander,
Dodging the H2O holes,
All sodden, like
Overcooked pasta.
Spitting out salty lungfuls
Of mild profanity,
And tight lipped
Objection.

The tree outside
The window
Doesn't object to
The sheen and glean,
As the leaves glimmer with
Messages of ecology,
And shimmer
With the dodgy-wire
Thermostat of global warming.
Sipping cocktails of
Atmosphere and pollution.
There are worse ways.

I gaze at trails of
Angel tears
Cascading down my window pane,
And wonder if you
Ever cried
And thoughts and thoughts
And thoughts of

How and why,
And greyness paints away
The pictures in the sky.

I just want to see
The clouds again.
For airy, balmy days of
Gentle blue and baby powder
White.
Faces brushed with breezes,
Delicate breaths
Of a lover,
And affections kissed
By the subtle smile of
A springtime sunrise.

But it's peaceful here.
The tree, the rain, Me.

SAD EYES

You say I have sad eyes, today…

That I am not here, there;
No kissing humour with
Sincere smiles.
But I am somewhere.
Maybe this world
Expects too much,
When my skin
Is wafer thin
And my heart feels the falter in
Humanity's tacit pulse.
Maybe I was built
For glass houses,
And I most certainly
Don't throw stones
At fragile egos.

I am not here,
There, not
Paying homage to
Polished and preened.
But I am somewhere.
Maybe this world
Expects too much,
When my eyes are
Dreary with monochrome
Skies,
And my mind is full
Of what's and why's.
Maybe I was built
For under the sea

Sarah Drury

And I most certainly
Delight in
Dreaming away
In reverie,
Beneath the moon's
Alluring tides.

I am not here,
There, not
Falling victim to
Wearisome woes
Of the worrisome world.
But I am somewhere.

Maybe this world
Expects too much,
When I'm just tired
Of being
A sigh in the breath
Of the lungs of
This mortal machine.
And my heart
Beats in rhythm
With fantasy,
Maybe I was built
For fairytales,
And I most certainly
Delight in
Being enchanted in
A cynical world.

You say I have
Sad eyes, today....

SATELLITE

It was traumatic.
A flick of a finger.
One soul left,
Another left soulless.
You soared, my love,
To wherever the universe
Assigned you conscious.
And I remained,
Screaming at Providence,
All waterfall eyed,
And treacherous tongued.
Fists plucking blasphemies,
Like expletive cherries
From a stone-heart punnet.

Detoxing from
The intrusive ebb and flow.
Silence mourning
Take-a-breath machines
And beat-your-heart regimes.
Quiet descends
In the precarious gap
Between hope
And dreams,
And hoped and dreamt
mocked cruelly
At hearts
Sitting on the ledge,
Naked and kissed
By the nonchalance
Of an ill wind.

Your body lifeless.
Alabaster flesh
Calls cruelly.
"Hold me!
Hold me!"
Sapphire eyes gaze
With sightless vision.
You are
Shattered like
A broken satellite,
Who can never
Circumnavigate my world,
Again.

SAY

So much to say
To you,
But
So much I
Can't say.

My tongue, it drips
In words as mute
As echoes
In a blizzard
Of silent
Hush hush whispers.

My mind hurts
With the constant
Cognitive constriction,
Minding my manners
And
Deluding my desires
In cloaks
Of decency.

I want the luxury
Champagne,
But the bubbles
Burst like
Insignificant dreams
Tumbling down
A heartbreak hill.
My tongue knows only
The taste of solitude,
And it is

So lonely,
Sitting in the night
With one glass only.

If only I could speak,
But I can't.
I am a mute,
In a landscape of
Hollow hearts.

SHOULD BE

4am.
Should be fast
Asleep.
Hate this.

My mind has
Its own mind.
It doesn't want
To slumber.
It takes a goldfish
In an ocean,
To fill my head
With what ifs?
Who whys? and
How
Will this end?

My pencil takes
The weight of
A heart so
Light, it
Draws my unsettled
Psyche in artistic form,
As hollow eye,
Naked folk,
Avert my gaze
On my iPad screen.

And I am
Vulnerable,
In my sleepless world.
Counting sheep who

Know no numbers.
Counting clocks
Who chide in circles.
Counting minutes
Til the sun high fives
The moon.

4am.
Should be fast
Asleep.
Hate this.

SINGLE MUM

I know I am
Your single mum.
Your friends have
Dads and you tell me
Often, that
You feel like
A stranger in your
Own social circle.
It must be hard to
Be a leper in
A land of dual
Parenting,
And paternal genetics.
Happy, wholesome
Smiling family snaps,
When you live in
A testosterone
Depleted zone.

It wasn't always
Faux joy selfies,
Just the two of us.
Conquering the world
With our Colgate smiles
And mum-son
Bonding.
Looking like
The world was made
For just us two,
And fleeting glimpses
Cannot magic
Fathers' faces

On iPhone imagery.

I am not in
The land of
Mice nor men.
If I could conjure up
The ideal role model,
I would paint your
Life with
Gentle men and
Honest souls,
And the heart of
a saintly martyr.
Knights fighting fearsome
Dragons and
Brave soldiers
(camouflaged anxiety)
Dedicating their lives
To an ethical cause.

I cannot raise
Fathers from the dead.
It is hard enough to
Keep memories alive
When they are stored
Deep within my mind,
And not yours.
But one day you
Will understand that
Once upon a time,
There were three
Of us.
Not this brave
Little duet

STRANGE

I must be strange.
That weird girl.
Covid raging,
People dying.
Maybe I shut out
The reality.
Maybe my eyes
See only the beauty
In the world,
When I should weep
And mourn
The ugliness.
But how can I
Bear to paint
Black
That which sets
Free my soul,
As I bask in
The light?
My ears may
Not hear the cries
Of trauma,
But my soul does,
And I paint them
Silent,
And pen them into
Translucent echoes.

I must be strange.
That weird girl.
Covid raging,
People dying.

Maybe I shut out
The reality.
Maybe my heart
Sees only the goodness
In the world,
When I should pray
And cry for
The desperation.
But how can I
Bear to sing,
In rhythms of dissonance,
That which sets
Free my heart,
As I dance in
The light.
My soul may not
Dance with
Demons,
But my mind
Sees,
And I shut my eyes,
And paint the pictures,
And write the words,
And live in
My kaleidoscope bubble.

SUN KISSED

Nice to see the sun today,
Painting golden hopes on
Hearts,
Of people
I have never known.
Breathing optimism into
Brooding woes of
Steel and stone.

Streets look different,
When shimmers of sunlight
Dance on swathes of noncommittal
Asphalt grey,
Ricocheting wildly
Like two hearts playing
Kiss Catch
In a teasing, beguiling
Way.

People smile,
When they are swathed
In golden haze,
And feel the healing warmth
On their naked skin.
They trade their pain
For emotional memories
They can store
This happy, happy in.

And I bask in serenity.

SWALLOWED

I think the ocean has
Swallowed me whole,
Today.

Sinking, sinking,
To my watery abode.

I feel comfortable here,
Lungs lilting in lament.
Singing songs of salt
And sadness.
Operas of alone,
For the afflicted
And deranged.

It's tough when your
Demeanor is rough,
And you toy with
The sharks,
And then laugh when
You're bitten.
Pain again,
Am I mad, am I sane?
Blood flows,
Pulse slows,
Thoughts go
Away.

I think the ocean
Has swallowed me whole,
Today.

SWIFTS

Paint me a sky
As it drifts into sleep.
And we sit here,
Generations apart,
Tied by a moment
In breath and beauty.
Me with my childlike
Sense of wonder.
You, with your heroic
Call of duty.

Times change.
But tonight
The clocks are timeless.
Graceful swifts
Command on wing
The centre stage.
Never hesitant,
Nor fearful of
Calamity.
Too beautiful
To be nature's circus.
God's opera
Whispered across the echoes
Of an ultramarine sky.

I didn't know it
Then.
Those warm summer nights,
Predicting the future
Of history.
And here I am

Forty years since.
Making wings
With memories.
How swift is time.

TEARS

Don't want to write
A sad poem,
But my eyes
Refuse to cooperate
With my
Polite smile,
And weather worn
Bravado.

Feelings are seeping out
Of closets
Where I thought
I had sealed doors with
Art and beautiful music.
Thinking I had grown beyond
The tears.
But I hadn't.
And haven't.

I saw a homeless man
Yesterday.
His face a map of pain
And dejection.
And today the black girl
On TV,
With eyes that
Sold a charity,
And broke me.

And my tears feel like
Insignificance.
Like a first world indulgence.

Privilege.

But I miss you.

TEDDY

You may be thirteen.
But teddy needs to hold your hand,
When he feels alone and afraid.
When the nights are dark and
Your room dances
With the ghosts of ghosts.
He hears the sinister whispers
Of the monsters
Under the bed,
And you say he's hearing things.
That monsters don't exist
And you hold his little paw
And sing
Nonsense.
And you both feel free.

Sarah Drury

THIRTEEN

I know you are almost thirteen.
You think the clock is
A conspiracy theory.
Dragging out the seconds
Until puberty grabs you
In a cool bro' embrace.

I can't count the minutes
You have lost
To my insanity.
Visits
To that funny place I go to stay
When mascara lashes weep into panda eyes,
And lips so red that the words
Tumble out as haemoglobin apologies.

The seconds you have lost
To my instability!
Always weak,
When I'm trying to weld hearts with girders.
Always sobbing crystalline tears
Into spun silk pillows,
Yet melting stainless steel with
The crimson heat of yours.

I don't expect medals and accolades
For being mediocre.
I just want you to know
That mummy tried.
She really tried.

TODAY

Will today be
An amnesty?
Or will it be
War torn Bosnia.

I slept,
But soldiers marched
In predatory legions.

I am prisoner
In my freedom.
My chains are
Screams and
Tantrums.

Everywhere I turn,
I see,
I hear,
I feel,
The cries of your war
Resounding off
My resilience.

They don't know
How I cope.
Nor do I.
But my life
Is always written
In chapters of
Better tomorrows.

And I hope.

And pray.

VAN GOGH WHORE

Tousled yellow
Paint,
Plays on alpha,
And omega.
Makes
Her smile.
Sunflowers,
Optimistic powers,
Self-expression,
Paint-licked hours.
Social media towers
Over her ego.
Always purloining the
Public
For a like.
Prostituting her art,
Like a
Cheap imitation
Van Gogh
Whore.

Sarah Drury

ABOUT THE AUTHOR

Sarah Drury lives in the North of England, in a working-class town. She is a retired teacher and is studying for a Bachelor of arts degree in painting.

Her poetry has evolved over the past several years and become more personal and introspective. It reflects her role as a mother, her experience of life, and her sensitive and empathic nature.

Her days are filled with beautiful music and inspirational art, as she pours her heart into her poetry.

Sarah Drury

Printed in Great Britain
by Amazon

69959475R00052